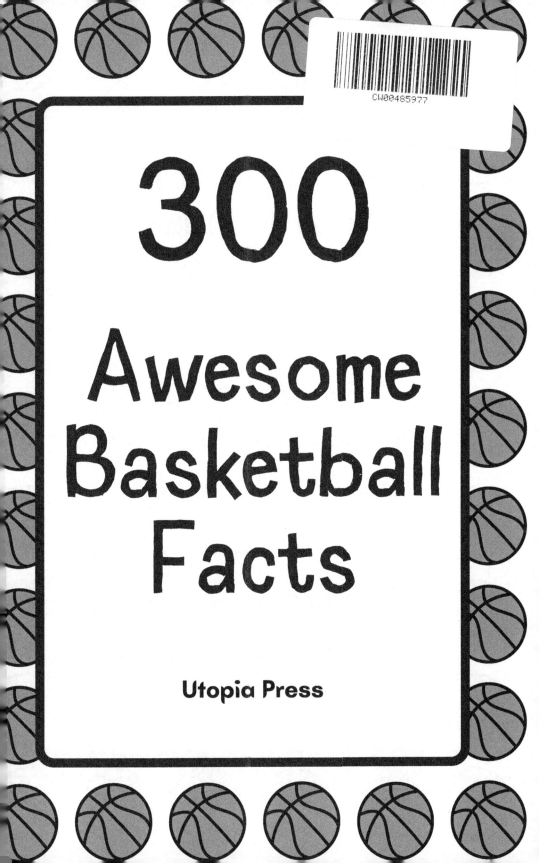

300

Awesome Basketball Facts

Utopia Press

The first National Basketball Association (NBA) game took place in 1946.

Founded in 1923, Sacramento Kings is the oldest NBA team ever.

Only 7,090 people were at the first game of the NBA in 1946.

The Celtics and Lakers have won the NBA 17 times in their history.

Bill Russell has the most NBA championship rings, with 11 rounds in just 13 years of playing for the Boston Celtics.

Kobe Bryant has missed the most times by any other player in the history of the NBA.

3-time NBA Champion Shaq O'Neal has missed 5,300 free throws in his career.

Golden State Warriors holds the record for most wins by a team in a single season with 73 wins and only nine losses during the 2015-16 season.

Wilt Chamberlain's 100 points are the most scored by any player in one game.

Stephen Curry has recorded the most three-pointers made by a player, with 3390 three-pointers.

Over 120 foreign players from forty countries were featured during the 2022-23 season.

Hank Biasatti was the first-ever international player in the league in 1946.

The all-time leading scorer in the history of the NBA with 38,652 points is Lebron James.

Micheal Jordan has never lost an NBA final in his career, with six final wins out of six.

Only two games have been played on Christmas Eve in over seventy years.

Lebron has been part of nineteen All-Star games consecutively since 2004.

Russel Westbrook has the most triple-doubles in NBA history.

Baron Davis currently has the record for the longest shot in the history of the NBA, with 89 feet in 2001.

The Philadelphia Warriors won the first-ever NBA title in 1946-47, now known as Golden State Warriors.

Kevin Garnett holds the record for most rebounds made by a single player in his career in the history of the NBA.

Wilt Chamberlain has the most rebounds made in a single game since 1960, with 55 rebounds.

Dwight Howard and Shaquille O'Neal hold the record for most dunks in the history of the NBA.

Karl Malone has made the most free throws in the NBA history with 9787 free throws.

Stephen Curry has the highest free throw percentage in the league's history.

Andre Drummonds holds the record for missing the most free throws in a single game with 23 misses.

Each team in the NBA plays 82 games in a regular season without the playoffs.

James Harden holds the record for missing the most three points in a career.

The Chicago Bulls won 6 NBA championships in seven seasons from 1991 to 1998.

The most assists in NBA history, with 15,806 assists, is by John Stockton.

Micheal Jordan holds the record for scoring the most points by a single player in a playoff game.

The 2019 NBA finals rings are the biggest and most expensive.

Boston Celtics hold the record for most conference titles with 22 in the history of the NBA.

Hakeem Olajuwon made 3830 total blocks in his career for an all-time record that is yet to be beaten.

The Toronto Raptors have blocked the most shots by a team in a game up against the Atalanta Hawks in 2001.

Wilt Chamberlain has the record for the most 50-point games during his career.

At 18 years and six days, Andrew Bynum is the youngest player ever in the NBA.

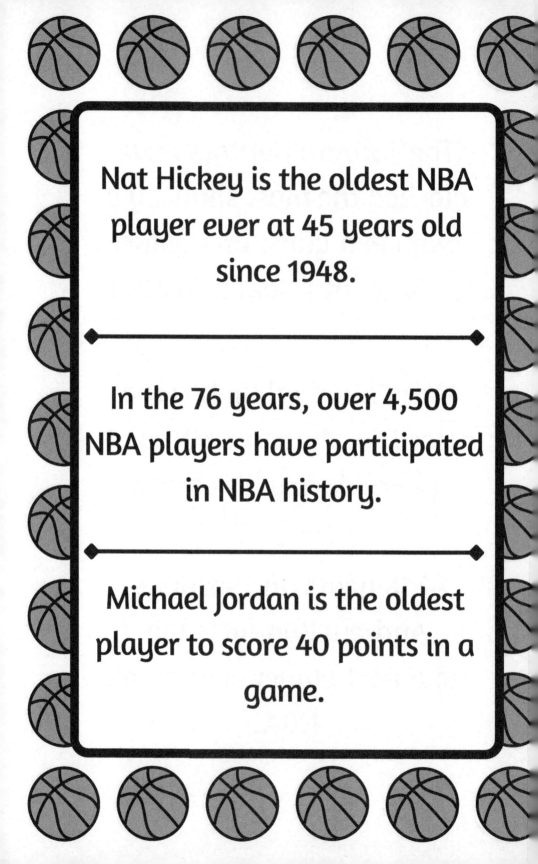

Nat Hickey is the oldest NBA player ever at 45 years old since 1948.

In the 76 years, over 4,500 NBA players have participated in NBA history.

Michael Jordan is the oldest player to score 40 points in a game.

The first-ever edition of the NBA only featured 11 teams compared to 30 teams as of today.

Sacramento Kings holds the record for not appearing in playoffs for 16 seasons straight.

The Boston Celtics hold the longest consecutive NBA Finals appearance streak with ten appearances between 1957 and 1966.

Boston Celtics won the record 8 NBA Finals in a row in 76 years of the league's history.

Allen Iverson is the lightest and shortest player to win the NBA MVP award.

Lebron James holds the record for losing most games in NBA finals since 1963.

The Los Angeles Lakers have made the most NBA finals in the league's history.

Cleveland Cavaliers won their first NBA title in 2016, defeating the Golden State Warriors.

The Los Angeles Clippers have never reached an NBA final.

Denver Nuggets won their first NBA game in 2023, defeating Miami Heat.

Robert Parish holds the record for playing the most games in the NBA with 1611 game appearances by a single player.

Kareem Abdul Jabbar has the most NBA MVP awards, with six.

Toronto Raptors won their first NBA championship in 2019.

1998-99 is the shortest NBA season ever, with only 50 games played by each team.

The 2020 NBA season was the only season played with no crowd due to the pandemic.

AC Green holds the record for the longest NBA streak without missing a game with an amazing 1,192 games.

The Philadelphia Sixers hold the record for losing 28 games in a row in two years.

There has never been an NBA team with an undefeated regular season.

The Minnesota Timberwolves hold the record of worst win-loss record since 1946.

The Detroit Pistons and Denver Nuggets hold the record for the highest-scoring NBA game, which Detroit won with only two points.

Memphis Grizzlies holds the record for the highest margin win by any team with a difference of 79 points against the Oklahoma Thunders.

The first player to have his signature shoe in history was Walt Clyde Frazier.

Micheal Jordan is the first NBA player to become a billionaire.

Stephen Curry is the highest-paid NBA player, with $52 million annually.

Golden State Warriors won their fourth title after 50 years in 2015.

Golden State Warriors hold the record for best record in a regular season with 73 wins and nine losses.

The record for most NBA championships by a coach is held by Phil Jackson with 11 championships.

Dennis Rodman holds the record for being the oldest player in NBA history to be first in the league for rebounds.

The Dallas Mavericks won their only NBA title in 2011.

Bill Russel is the only player in NBA history whose jersey number was retired by all NBA teams.

Boston Celtics is the only NBA team with the most retired jersey numbers, with 25 leading from the front.

In honor of Michael Jordan, The Chicago Bulls and Miami Heat retired the number 23, but Jordan never played for Miami.

The only player in NBA history with two retired numbers is Kobe Bryant.

Paul Gasol, an NBA hall of famer, went to Medical School.

Michael Jordan won his first NBA MVP award at the age of 25.

Micheal Jordan averaged 28.2 points per game and won the Rookie of the Year in his first season.

Karl Malone is the oldest NBA player to win the MVP award at 35.

The youngest player to have won an NBA Finals MVP is Magic Johnson.

Darko Milicic is the youngest player ever to win an NBA ring.

Toronto Raptors joined the NBA in 1995.

The Sacramento Kings wear the crown as the oldest NBA franchise, founded in 1923.

Kareem Abdul Jabbar holds the record for most career wins in the playoffs and regular season with 1,228 wins.

The Chicago Bulls won their first NBA championship in 1991.

San Antonio Spurs won five NBA championships with the same coach.

In 2006, the Miami Heat won their first Championship.

Milwaukee Bucks won their first-ever Championship in 1971.

Golden State Warriors relocated from Philadelphia to San Francisco in 1962 and changed its name in 1971.

The New Jersey Nets changed their name to Brooklyn Nets during relocation in 2012.

The Los Angeles Lakers and L.A. Clippers have the same arena for their home games.

The Washinton Wizards won their only NBA championship in 1978.

Since 1891, the standard basketball hoop stands 10ft tall.

The highest-rated and most-watched NBA Finals series is the 1998 NBA Finals.

The 2023 NBA playoffs earned eight billion views across social media, making it the most watched ever.

Steve Kerr won 5 NBA rings as a player and four as a coach.

Bill Russell won 9 NBA championships as a player.

Wilt Chamberlain has the most records named to any basketball player, holding 72 different records.

Kareem Abdul Jabbar won his first NBA ring with the Milwaukee Bucks 1971.

Milwaukee Bucks won their second Championship after 50 years in 2021.

Giannis Antetokounmpo became the first ever NBA player to get 200 points, 100 rebounds, and 50 assists in a single series.

Nikola Jokic is the first player in the history of the NBA to have a triple-double in the NBA finals.

The first player in NBA history to get at least 10,000 points, 10,000 rebounds, and 10,000 assists is Lebron James.

The average NBA career lasts around 4.5 years.

To this day, only six other players have reached 30,000 points in a single career.

Dennis Smith Jr. has the highest vertical jump of all current NBA players, with a reach of 48 inches.

Kobe Bryant scored an astonishing 81 points in a single game.

Klay Thompson has the most 3-pointers in one game.

John Lucas has the most assists in a game with exactly 0 points, with 24 assists.

LeBron has seven game-winning shots for 19 seasons of play.

Kevin Durant posted his most points in a game versus the Hawks with 55 points.

LeBron James had one game played with exactly 0 assists in 2012 against the Celtics.

Steph Curry's best career high is 62 points for a single game.

The Cleveland Cavaliers won after losing three games in the NBA Finals 2016.

In 1988, the Detroit Pistons were nicknamed "The Bad Boys."

The Boston Celtics and New York Knicks are the only teams that never moved.

Los Angeles has the most hall-of-fame players in the NBA.

The Lakers were founded in Minneapolis.

The Lakers have the first female controlling owner.

The Los Angeles Lakers, along with The Boston Celtics, have played in the NBA Finals a record 12 times together.

1980s Lakers were nicknamed "Showtime."
The third pick for the 2003 NBA draft was Carmelo Anthony, along with Lebron James.

Jokic ranks as the lowest draft pick (41st) to win Finals MVP.

Nikola Jokic is the first player selected outside the top 15 to win both Finals MVP and regular-season MVP.

Hall-of-Famer Kobe Bryant won the All-Star MVP award a record four times in his career.

John Havlicek was unbeaten in the NBA Finals with a record of 8-0.

Charles Barkley never won a single NBA championship in his whole career.

Reggie Miller is regarded by many as the best clutch 3-point shooter.

Lebron James has the most 4th quarter points in NBA history.

Golden State scored a league-record 55 first-quarter points in the history of the NBA.

No basketball team has ever scored 200 points in a professional game.

LeBron James had his most shot attempts in a game against the Raptors in 2006.

Phoenix set the NBA record for the most points scored by a team in the first half, with 107 points.

The record for most assists in a game, with 30 assists, belongs to Scott Skiles.

Lebron James is the fastest NBA player to score 5000 points in an NBA career.

Jason Tatum is the youngest NBA player to hit 1,000 threes at 24.

Micheal Jordan's nickname was "Black Jesus" during the 90's era.

Indiana Pacers never won a National Championship in NBA history.

Shaquille O'Neal made more money after retirement than in his entire NBA career.

From 2000 to 2004, the La Lakers dominated the NBA with three Championships and one runner-up.

Hakeem Olajuwon holds the record for the most blocks in NBA history with 3,830 blocks.

The Houston Rockets won back-to-back NBA championships in 1994 and 1995.

Stephen Curry has won four NBA championships in his career.

Kawhi Leonard helped the Toronto Raptors win their first-ever NBA championship in 2019.

Michael Jordan has never lost an NBA final in his career.

Kobe Bryant scored 60 points in his last-ever game against the Utah Jazz.

Stephen Curry holds the record for most 3-point attempts made in history.

Karl Malone has the most free throw attempts in NBA history.

Kareem Abdul Jabbar holds the record for most minutes played in the history of the NBA, with 57,446 minutes.

Michael Jordan scored 32,292 points in his whole NBA career.

The New York Knicks have two NBA Championships in their franchise history.

Charles Barkley won the 1993 NBA MVP award, beating Michael Jordan.

Lebron James has the most NBA All-Star appearances, with 19 in a 20-year career.

Lebron James debut NBA game was against the Sacramento Kings scoring 25 points.

Los Angeles Lakers George Mikan is considered one of the best centers in NBA history.

The 1992 Dream Team is known as the best USA basketball team of all time.

Micheal Jordan has 2 Olympic gold medals.

Ben Wallace is widely speculated as the worst free-throw shooter point shooter in NBA history.

Young Dwayne Wade won his first NBA title in 2006.

Lebron James is a 4-time NBA MVP award winner.

The Los Angeles Laker's famous Staples Center is now known as Crypto Arena.

Magic Johnson won his first NBA ring in his rookie year.

Larry Bird was 24 years old when he won his first NBA championship.

Tim Duncan has five NBA Championships with the Spurs.

Reggie Miller never won an NBA championship in his whole career.

In 1996, Magic Johnson made a shocking retirement.

Isiah Thomas won three NBA titles with the Detroit Pistons.

Michael Jordan started his career playing for North Carolina Tar Heels as a freshman.

Allen Iverson never won a single NBA championship in his 20-year career.

The 1998 NBA finals are the most-seen NBA final ever in history.

Bird and Magic shared a great rivalry during the 1980's era.

Chicago Bulls have not won a NBA championship since 1998.

Dennis Rodman once appeared in a WCW event during the 1990's era.

L.A. Lakers have 26 players in the Hall of Fame.

Michael Jordan owns the Charlotte Hornets.

Yao helped build bridges between the U.S. and China through sports with lasting results.

Miami Heat was established in 1988.

Andy Phillip recorded the first triple-double in NBA history for the Philadelphia Warriors in 1950.

Lebron James won his 3rd NBA title in his hometown, Cleveland.

Tyson Curtis, aka Muggsy, is the shortest known NBA player with 5ft 3in.

Jimmy Butler has never won an NBA championship in his career.

Vince Carter holds the record of playing 22 seasons, the longest of any other NBA player.

Karl Malone has never won any NBA championship in his career.

Jerry West only won one time out of nine NBA finals he played with the L.A. Lakers.

Lebron James has over 150 million followers on Instagram, the most of any other NBA player.

Manute Bol is the tallest player in the history of the NBA at 7ft 6in.

Micheal Jordan was drafted 3rd overall in 1984 for the Chicago Bulls.

Kobe Bryant won the NBA All-Star Game MVP award four times.

Dennis Rodman is known as the best rebounding forward in NBA history.

Wang Zhizhi was the first Chinese player in NBA history selected by Dallas Mavericks.

Jordan's first NBA deal with the Chicago Bulls paid him $6.3 million over seven years.

The 2019-20 Denver Nuggets are the only NBA team to return from a 3-1 series deficit multiple times in the same year.

African countries have 42 NBA players, including 30 from Nigeria.

Moses Malone & Bill Walton were the first players to earn $1 Million in a season.

Reggie Harding skipped college in 1962 and went straight from high school into the world's toughest basketball league.

Allen Iverson began using basketball sleeves during the 2000-01 season, which became a global fashion style.

Kobe Bryant broke Pennsylvania's state record of 2,883 points in high school.

Oscar Benjamin scored the first basket in the Basketball Association of America.

Scottie Pippen had nine appearances in the Conference Finals in his career.

The longest winning streak, including playoff games in Golden State Warriors history, is 27 games.

The Philadelphia 76ers have the longest losing streak of regular season games in NBA history at 28 straight games.

Bryant ranked third on the NBA list for points in his career in December 2014.

The 2015-16 Cleveland Cavaliers are the only team to return after being down 3-1 in the NBA Finals and win Game 7.

The San Antonio Spurs hold the highest win–loss record percentage in NBA History.

Shaq, in 1996, was named to the National Basketball Association (NBA) list of 50 greatest players.

The Los Angeles Lakers won 33 straight games in the 1971–72 season.

Vince Carter has lost the most career games, with 756 losses.

The 1994-95 Houston Rockets were the lowest-seeded team to win the NBA Finals.

Lebron James' longest shot is 83 feet.

The Fort Wayne Pistons narrowly beat the Minneapolis Lakers 19-18 in 1950 to make it the lowest-scoring game in NBA history.

The Los Angeles Laker's worst season was 2014-15 with a 17-65 record.

Twelve NBA teams have never won a championship.

The team to have the most conference titles, with 19, is the Los Angeles Lakers.

Bill Russel won 11 conference titles out of 11.

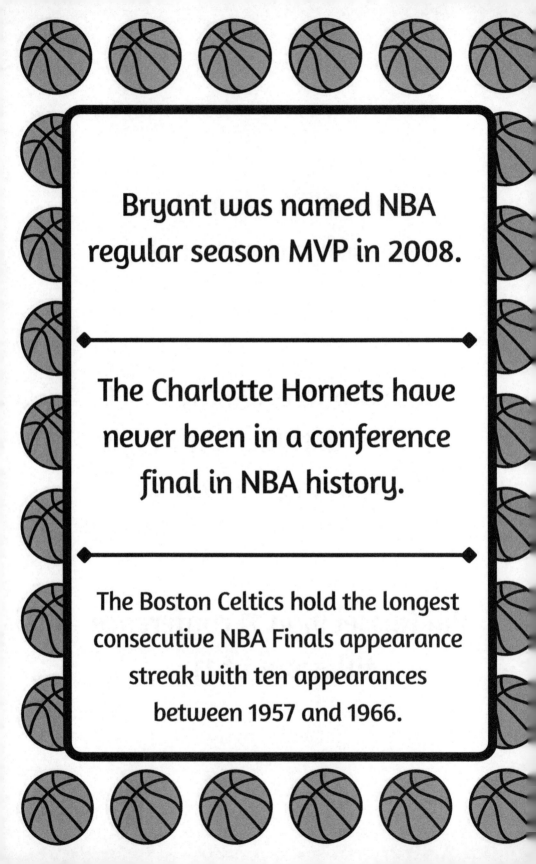

Bryant was named NBA regular season MVP in 2008.

The Charlotte Hornets have never been in a conference final in NBA history.

The Boston Celtics hold the longest consecutive NBA Finals appearance streak with ten appearances between 1957 and 1966.

Bill Rusell won 8 NBA championships in a row from 1959 to 1966.

Charlotte Hornets selected Kobe Bryant as the 13th overall pick.

LeBron James has 12 appearances in the Conference Finals in his career.

Since the 1980 season, one of the two No. 1 seeds has won the NBA championship 22 times.

The 1994 Sonics were the first No. 1 seed to lose the first round of NBA playoffs.

Asian American point guard Wat Misaka broke basketball's color barrier as the first non-white player in the NBA in 1947.

Shaquille O'Neal won the MVP award once in his career.

Michael Jordan won 3 championships without Scottie Pippen in his career.

Spencer Hayward sued the NBA in 1971 to break the 4-year graduation law.

Six teams have overcome a 2–0 deficit in NBA playoff history.

Shaquille O'Neal is one of only three players to have won All-Star game MVP, NBA MVP, and Finals MVP honors in the same year.

Kobe Bryant was the youngest All-Star Game player in 1998.

LeBron James writes and eats with his left hand.

There has never been a quintuple double in the NBA.

Paul Pierce was stabbed eleven times and still managed to play every game in the 2000-01 season.

Boban Marjanovic of the L.A Clippers is the heaviest player in the league, weighing 290 lbs.

The Orlando Magic had the lowest scoring output of any team game in the 2018/19 NBA season.

The average NBA player stands 79 inches tall (6' 7") and weighs about 220 pounds.

George Yardley scored a phenomenal 2001 points for the Detroit Falcons in the 1957-1958 season.

The Toronto Huskies were Toronto's First NBA team and one of the first teams in the league.

Michael Jordan was fined $5,000 for every game he wore Air Jordans as his shoes violated league policy.

The highest-paid cheerleaders in the NBA belong to the New York Knicks, with a per-match fee of $650.

Shaq played for the Los Angeles Lakers, Boston Celtics, Cleveland Cavaliers, Orlando Magic, Phoenix Suns, and Miami Heat in his 19 NBA seasons.

The silhouette in the NBA logo is former Los Angeles Laker Jerry West.

Kareem Abdul-Jabbar managed to only make one 3-point shot in his entire 20-year career.

Oscar Robertson averaged a triple-double for a season as a second-year NBA player for the Cincinnati Royals in 1962.

The only Finals the Celtics ever lost with Bill Russell was to the Bob Pettit-led team St. Louis Hawks in 1958, four games to two.

Jerry West won the first MVP award ever in NBA history.

Michael Jordan and Lebron James share the record for being the only NBA players to win a regular-season MVP, NBA Finals MVP, & Olympic gold medal in the same year.

In 1951, the longest NBA game lasted 78 minutes.

The biggest whooping in NBA history was when the Cleveland Cavaliers destroyed the Miami Heat 148-80 in 1991.

Chris Ford of the Boston Celtics is widely credited with making the first three-point shot in the history of the NBA.

Kawhi Leonard is just the third player in NBA league history to win Finals MVP with multiple teams.

The NBA 2K Franchise by Take-Two Interactive is the best-selling Basketball series.

Larry Bird is the only NBA player to win coach, executive, and MVP of the year.

There are only six teams in the 72-year history of the league to have made it to four straight Finals.

The NBA named a Most Valuable Player in the finals for the first time in 1969.

Stephen Curry's ten career games with double-digit three-pointers are the most by any player in the history of the NBA.

The youngest player to have won an NBA championship is Darko Milicic.

Robert Parish is the oldest player to have won an NBA championship.

The Los Angeles Lakers have been to the playoffs 60 times in 70 seasons - the most in NBA history.

The great Michael Jordan's net worth is estimated to be roughly 2 Billion dollars.

From March 24, 1993, to November 9, 1993, The Detroit Pistons' Michael Williams connected with the bottom of the net on 97 free throws in a row.

The Utah Jazz managed to get whistled for 52 fouls in a 119-115 loss to the Phoenix Suns.

Michael Jordan was the first player in league history to receive 2,000,000+ votes.

The very first slam dunk contest was held in 1976 in Denver at the American Basketball Association All-Star game.

Michael Jordan was the most popular NBA player nine times.

At 285 pounds, Zion Williamson is the 2nd heaviest player in the NBA.

Gregg Popovich (San Antonio Spurs) is the oldest current NBA coach at 69 years old.

Only four players have six or more NBA Rings.

2019's number 1 draft pick, Zion Williamson, can dunk from the free-throw line.

The Washington NBA team, originally known as the "Bullets," changed their name to the "Wizards".

The Memphis Grizzlies lost a game by 61 points last season - the sixth-worst blowout in NBA history.

Wilt Chamberlain became the first ever NBA player to earn $100,000 in salary in 1965.

The Miami Heat paid seven players $10 million or more in the 2018/19 season, the most in the NBA.

The NBA stated that it will no longer be testing for marijuana use in the off-season.

The highest salary in the WNBA is $242,154 compared to over $52 million in the NBA.

In the last 30 years, eight teams have won the NBA Championship.

NBA Hall of Famer great Bill Russell became the very first African-American head coach to win a championship.

In 2019, Dwyane Wade became the only player in NBA history to get a triple-double in his final career game against the Brooklyn Nets.

Magic Johnson was the first player to receive 1,000,000+ NBA All-Star votes.

In 73 editions, only 14 coaches have won more than one NBA Championship.

Karl-Anthony Towns led the NBA with 68 double-doubles in the 2018-19 season.

Pelicans' Zion Williamson had the highest max vertical leap in Duke history.

Michael Jordan never lost more than two games in a row from November 1990 until he retired from the Bulls in 1998.

Draymond Green is the only player in history to get a triple-double without scoring ten points.

NBA MVP Hakeem Olajuwon released his own $35 sneaker instead of endorsing shoes from Nike in 1994.

Whilst hobbling on a sprained ankle, Isiah Thomas somehow scored an NBA-record 25 points in the third quarter.

Wilt Chamberlain averaged 37.6 points per game in his rookie year playing for the Philadelphia Warriors.

Magic Johnson recorded the most career triple-doubles in the playoffs, with thirty as a member of the Los Angeles Lakers.

Kobe Bryant met his wife, Vanessa, on the set of a video by Tha Eastsidaz.

Isiah Thomas scored 16 points in 94 seconds and still lost during the 1984 playoffs.

Kobe Bryant was the 13th draft pick in the 1996 NBA draft.

Wilt Chamberlain spent just one year with the Harlem Globetrotters team – and on March 9, 2000, they retired his No. 13.

The Toronto Raptors are the first team over the past 50 seasons to make it to the NBA Finals without a single top-10 pick on its roster.

If you are a 7+ foot tall American male between the ages of 20 and 40, there is a 17% chance you currently play for the NBA.

Tim Duncan made the all-NBA defense team 15 times, which is a record.

In the last game of the 2012 season, Golden State Warriors started five rookies in a game for an NBA record.

Nikola Jokic got the fastest triple-double in NBA history with fourteen minutes and thirty-three seconds in 2018.

Michael Jordan's Air Jordan 11 is regarded as the best-selling and top NBA shoe of all time.

NBA salaries vary greatly, but the average player makes around $8.5 million annually.

James Harden scored the highest number of points in a triple-double, with sixty in 2018 for the Houston Rockets.

LeBron James has recorded the most turnovers in NBA history, with 4966 and counting.

Michael Jordan scored 60-plus points five times in his career.

Stephen Curry is regarded by many as the greatest shooter in NBA history.

De'Aaron Fox was voted the fastest player with the ball in his hands by all NBA general managers for the 2021-22 season.

Tacko Fall has the longest wingspan of all current players, measuring 8 feet 4 inches.

Scan The QR Code To Check Out More Utopia Press Books On Amazon!

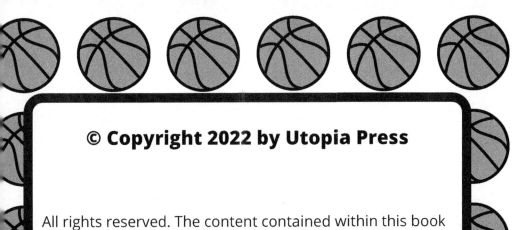

© Copyright 2022 by Utopia Press

All rights reserved. The content contained within this book may not be reproduced, duplicated or transmitted without direct written permission from the author or the publisher

ISBN: 9798864282335

Imprint: Independently published

For any questions or enquiries please email us and we would happily available to help and positive reviews and ratings are greatly appreciated

theutopiapress@gmail.com

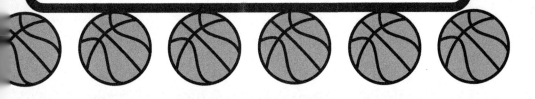

Printed in Great Britain
by Amazon

38431702R10059